FUNKY HAIR
AND
TRENDY LOOKS

Written by
LISA REGAN

Illustrated by
KATIE SAUNDERS

ARMADILLO

CONTENTS

LET'S GET FUNKY!	3
STARTING POINTS	4
EASY PEASY	6
IN A TWIST	7
FRESH FACED	8
ROUGH AND TUMBLE	9
BEADED BANDS	10
MAKEOVER MAGIC	11
CURLY WURLY	12
BUBBLY BUNCHES	13
TWIST AND SHOUT	14
LOOKING LIVELY	16
FUNKY ACCESSORIES	17

PLENTY OF PLAITS	18
TWO IN ONE	20
BIG HAIR	21
ON THE SIDE	22
FUN FOR FINGERS	23
FUN IN THE SUN	24
FUNKY GIRL	26
PARTY, PARTY	27
GET SET FOR SUMMER	28
MEHNDI MAGIC	29
CRAZY LADY	30
MERMAID BRAIDS	31
YOU GO, GIRL!	32

There is nothing too difficult in this book, but some hairstyles take a little bit of practice to get right. Look out for the flower code at the top of each style:

🌼 = super simple styles

🌼🌼 = need a little more practice

🌼🌼🌼 = a bit fiddly but well worth it.

LET'S GET FUNKY!

Are you the kind of girl who likes to look her best all the time? Or do you wait to wow everyone at special occasions such as parties? Whichever you are, this book is full of cool looks and handy hints for YOU.

Flick through the pages and you'll see a whole selection of fantastic hairstyles and new beauty tips for you to try out. Practise the make-up ideas and hairstyles on your own before a big party, or invite your friends round so that you can all experiment together.

Here are the basic things you'll need to get started:

HAIRBRUSHES

The best all-rounder is one with air-vents and soft plastic bristles. Always keep brushes and combs clean for super-shiny hair.

COMBS

Use a comb with a thin handle for partings and styling. If your hair is wet, use a wide-toothed comb, or you could damage your hair.

HAIRDRYER

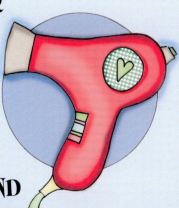

Only blow-dry your hair when you're doing a special style. Let your hair dry naturally whenever you can.

HAIRBANDS, BOBBLES AND CLIPS

Collect all sorts of styles and colours to jazz up your party hair! Never use ordinary elastic bands as they can break and tear your hair.

MAKE-UP AND NAIL VARNISH

Gather together a few different colours to experiment with. Glittery make-up and hair mascara are great for special occasions!

3

STARTING POINTS

No matter how you style your hair, if it's dirty and in bad condition, it won't look good. You don't have to spend a fortune to keep it shiny and healthy, though. Check out these easy-peasy rules for lovely locks!

SHORT CUTS

Find a hairdresser you like and have regular trims. If your hair is cut into a definite style, you'll need an appointment every six to eight weeks to keep it in shape. Even long hair needs to be trimmed every few months to get rid of damaged ends.

SQUEAKY CLEAN

Wash your hair at least every three days, and use conditioner each time. Good, cheaper brands are fine. With really expensive shampoo you're often paying extra for a designer name and expensive packaging. Follow the steps on the next page for a perfect hair wash!

♥ TOP TIP

Unless you have really greasy or dry hair, choose a shampoo and conditioner for frequent use on normal hair.

DON'T GO THERE!

Never cut your own fringe! It's not worth risking the embarrassment if it goes wrong, and there's a good chance that it will! If your fringe is getting in your eyes and you aren't due for a trim, choose a style that clips it away from your face.

FOOD FOR HAIR

For the healthiest hair ever, make sure you eat properly. If you don't get a balanced diet, with lots of fruit, vegetables, dairy products and protein, your hair will suffer. Try to drink lots of water, too, which benefits your hair and skin.

DE-GUNK

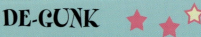

Don't overload your hair with mousse, gel, wax or hairspray. Only try one product at a time (never all of them at once) and use tiny amounts. It's easy to add a bit more but impossible to take any out of your hair without washing it and starting again.

1 Wet your hair thoroughly. Pour a coin-sized blob of shampoo into your palm and mix in a few drops of water to make it more liquid. You may need to use two blobs if your hair is very long or very dirty.

WASH AND GO!

For the cleanest, shiniest hair around, always wash your hair in the shower or under running water. If you simply lie in your bathwater to wet your hair, you're just coating it with bubble bath, soap and whatever dirt you've just washed off the rest of you!

2 Massage the shampoo through your hair, using your fingertips to get right to the roots. Wash away all the bubbles with clean water, and gently squeeze as much water as you can from your hair. One wash will be enough unless you've been busy on the sports' field or with your mousse and hairspray!

3 After shampooing, pour a blob of conditioner onto your palm (about the same size as the shampoo blob) and divide it between your two hands. Rub your hands over your whole head so that all your hair is evenly covered with conditioner.

4 Leave your hair for a couple of minutes before rinsing it thoroughly. If you can bear it, use very cool water for a final rinse to make your hair extra shiny. Some people add two drops of vinegar to a jugful of water for extra shine.

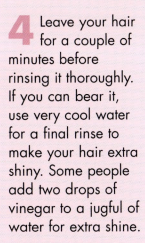

5 Wrap a towel around your hair and wait at least ten minutes before you comb or dry your hair. Don't rub madly at your hair with the towel, or you'll put back all the tangles that your conditioner helped take out!

EASY PEASY

Here are two simple styles to start with. They will be good practice for styling your hair. All you need are a hairbrush and a selection of coloured bobbles. Try the styles on a friend if you find it difficult to work on your own hair.

BOBBLICIOUS!

1 Brush your hair until it is smooth and falls down your back. Pull it all together at your neck so it's in one ponytail.

2 Wrap a hairband around and around the ponytail to hold it firmly in place. Brush the ponytail smooth.

3 Decorate the ponytail with two or three more bobbles further down. Space them out evenly to look super cool.

3-2-1

1 For a slightly different style, use just the top section of your hair to make a small ponytail and hold it in place with a bobble.

2 Make a second ponytail halfway down, around the first one.

3 Finally, gather all the rest of your loose hair and the main ponytail and use a bobble to hold them together at your neck.

IN A TWIST

This twisty-turny style is really easy to do, and gives practice in parting your hair. It should work even if you have a fringe, as long as you twist neatly and patiently! Your hair needs to reach to your shoulders (or longer) for the best effect.

1 Brush your hair smoothly back from your face. Run a comb or comb handle from front to back where you want your parting to be. Comb the hair away from the parting on each side.

2 Start with the side that has most hair (or either side with a centre parting). Gather together about 1cm at the front and twist it firmly. Add another 1cm section and twist both together.

3 Keep adding 1cm sections like this, working away from your parting, and twisting them all firmly together.

4 When the twist reaches the side of your face, keep twisting without adding more hair round to the back of your head. Hold the twist with a hair clip for the moment.

💜 TOP TIP
If your hair isn't long enough to twist right round to the back, use a pretty hairclip above each ear to hold the twists in place.

5 Start at the front again, twisting the other side. Work round to the back, unclip the first twist and twist the two pieces together. Hold them in place with a bobble.

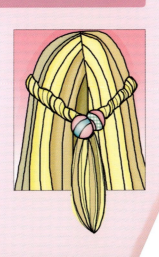

FRESH FACED

Like your hair, your skin will look its best if it's healthy and glowing. Piling make-up onto dull and lifeless skin won't help much. But don't panic if you get spots – you're not alone!

KEEP IT CLEAN

It's vital that you take off any make-up before you go to bed at night, to allow your skin to breathe and stop it getting greasy and dull. Use baby lotion to remove make-up, then splash warm water on your face until all the baby lotion has been washed away. Every couple of days, wash your face gently with warm water and a flannel to keep your skin sparkling clean. You shouldn't need to buy make-up remover and face creams until you're much older.

SEEING SPOTS

There isn't a girl in the world who hasn't had a spot at one time or another. But some people seem to be unlucky and get more than others. If you get lots of spots, especially if they seem to be under the surface of your skin, it may be acne. You should see a doctor if you're worried about something like this.

If you just get an occasional pimple, please remember the golden rule: LEAVE IT ALONE! Touching it might make it worse, or spread germs. Picking it will certainly not help and could leave a permanent scar. If a spot is really making you feel shy, dab a cotton bud in some foundation or concealer and dot it on the spot to take away some of the redness. Use a tiny dab of witch hazel or antiseptic on damp cottonwool to wipe it clean at bedtime.

ADDED EXTRAS

No matter how much money you spend on make-up and cosmetics, the best beauty products are free! Just make sure you get enough sleep, and your skin will glow, your eyes will sparkle, and you won't have dark circles under your eyes. Keep your teeth clean and healthy, with regular dental checks, for the best smile in town (without needing to wear lippy all the time).

ROUGH AND TUMBLE

This style works best if your hair has its own natural waviness, but use the top tip to make your own curls if your hair is super-straight. It's a great style for just hanging out with your friends.

1 Dampen your hair and scrunch a tiny amount of mousse through all your hair. (Only use a blob the size of a ping pong ball.)

2 Hang your head upside down and blast your hair for five minutes with a hairdryer, scrunching it in your hand as it dries.

♥ Top Tip
If your hair is too straight for this style, add some curl overnight. Dampen your hair and divide it into 8 to 16 sections. Wrap each section around a soft roller, a strip of material or even a fuzzy pipecleaner! Take these out the next morning, and you should have a head of girly curls.

3 Make a centre parting and pull each side into a low ponytail, fastening it with a little hairband. Don't brush or comb your hair, just use your fingers.

4 Wrap a small section of hair around each hairband to hide the band completely. Tuck in the loose ends, or hold them firmly with a hair grip.

BEADED BANDS

Here are some easy ways to add glitz and glamour to any length of hair. To make it easier to thread beads onto your hair, use a tiny amount of gel (or even just water) on the tips of the hair to "glue" all the ends together to make a point.

SHORT AND SPIKY

For short hair, use medium-sized beads and clear bands. Thread the band through the hole in the bead, then around a small piece of hair. Loop first one end of the band then the other over the bead to hold it in place.

BOBBY DAZZLER

If you're putting on the glitz for a party, splash out on some hair jewels. There are two types: some have velcro on the back, so they simply "stick" in place on smooth hair. The others have a wire spiral that winds down into the roots of your hair. Both types work best if your hair is swept up into a high ponytail or smart up-do.

YOU'VE BEEN FRAMED

Frame your face by leaving your hair loose and threading beads onto strands at the front. Comb one or two 1cm sections each side of your face. Slide the hair through the centre of a bead, and keep it in place by fixing a tiny, clear hairband underneath.

PRETTY PATIENT

This style takes patience but you don't need to use as many beads as shown here. Pull your hair up into a high ponytail and hold it in place with a hairband. Then take small strands of hair and thread beads onto them, fixing each in place as shown in You've Been Framed on the left. A little hair gel may help you.

10

MAKEOVER MAGIC

Your favourite pop stars don't wear masses of make-up all the time, especially if they're just popping out to the shops or to see friends. For young faces, the art of looking good is to apply small amounts of make-up carefully.

BACK TO BASICS

If you want to wear make-up that improves your looks but doesn't scream, "Look at how much make-up I'm wearing!", pick pale, pretty colours that are close to your skin colour.

Start with nice, clean skin (just splash water on your face and pat dry with a soft towel). Cover any spots that are bothering you (see page 8).

EYE, EYE

For daytime, keep eye make-up simple. Use a brush to apply one colour across your whole eyelid. Grey, cream, brown, pale blue, green or pink work well.

LOVELY LASHES

For the daytime, stick to plain brown or black mascara. One coat should be enough. For party make-up ideas, turn to pages 16 and 26.

LUSCIOUS LIPS

Choose a colour that's close to your natural lip colour. Instead of applying it straight from the tube, smudge on the colour with your fingertip. This presses it into your lips and makes it last longer. Kiss a tissue and dab on some more lippy. If you like, use a clear gloss on top to make your smile even more noticeable.

BLUSHING BEAUTY

Don't be scared of blusher – it's not hard to use, and it finishes your look perfectly. Cream blusher is easy to apply. Smudge one fingertip through the blusher and dab spots of colour onto your cheek. Start in front of your ear and make a line towards the bottom of your nose, following your cheek bone. Rub gently to blend the edges.

CURLY WURLY

If your hair is naturally curly, make the most of it instead of wishing it could be straighter. Avoid styles with a fringe, as it has a nasty habit of going frizzy and ruining your whole look.

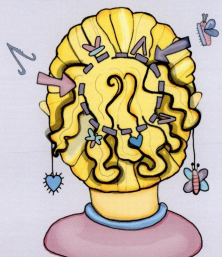

1 To make sure your hair dries with as many curls as possible, squirt a little serum onto the ends, or use your usual styling product for curls.

2 Comb all your hair away from your face. Instead of pulling your hair tightly into a hairband for a ponytail, use plain hair grips to hold sections of hair away from your face.

3 Position the grips in a rough circle, about the size of a CD. Once your hair is pinned tightly in place, and looks good from all sides, decorate around the edge of the circle with groovy grips.

4 If your hair won't stay secure like this, it may help to pull back small sections at a time and give each a single twist before fixing in place.

♥ **TOP TIP**
Experiment with this style, pinning your hair higher or lower on your head to suit your face.

BUBBLY BUNCHES

This style is soooooo simple to do but is really effective on crazy curls. For the best look, keep the bunches quite high up on your head, although check that this suits the shape of your face.

1 Make a parting, slightly off-centre, from your forehead to a point on top of your head, about level with your ears. Brush the remaining back section of hair backwards.

2 Add a little extra "oomph" to this back section of hair by back-combing it. Then make another parting in this section, continuing the first parting.

3 Pull each side of your hair, including the back-combed sections, into high bunches. Hold them in place with hair bobbles or hairbands. Fluff out the bunches a little.

4 Check in a mirror that your bunches are even and level. Scrunch a little hair serum or wax into the ends of the bunches for added curl and definition.

♥ Top Tip
To backcomb your hair, hold a section straight out from your head and comb it gently from the ends to the roots (instead of from the roots to the ends as you would usually do). This adds extra volume to your style. However, don't do it every day, as too much backcombing can damage your hair.

13

TWIST AND SHOUT

If you have lots of hair grips and clips, and a little time and patience, you can twist your hair into all sorts of cool styles. It doesn't matter if your hair is short, long or mid-length, as long as it will twist!

ON THE SIDE

1 Make a centre parting in your hair, and brush each side smooth behind your ears. Hold with clips if necessary.

2 Divide the left-hand side into two even sections, and put each in a ponytail held with a hairband.

3 Twist one section forwards a couple of times, and pin the ponytail back up to the bobble using hair grips.

4 Twist the other section backwards a couple of times, and pin this twist in place in the same way.

5 Repeat on the righthand side. Use hair wax to tease the ends into small funky spikes.

♥ Top Tip
To tidy up shorter hairs on your neckline that don't pull neatly into your bunches, spray a small amount of hairspray onto an old toothbrush and brush gently into place.

SHORT AND SWEET

If your hair is short on top, create pretty twists to frame your face and decorate them with cute clips. Make a short parting, just off-centre, and another one alongside, so you have a neat section of hair. Twist this section over and over, pulling it backwards slightly as you twist. Hold it firmly in place with a spring clip. Make more sections of the same size, and twist and clip each one as before. Add a little wax to the ends to spike up your hair.

LONG AND LOVELY

Twist longer hair in the same way, and it will look completely different! You don't need to make such neat partings this time. Simply gather up sections from the front of your hair, and twist them backwards, over and over again. Twist until they're about level with your ears. Clip each twist in place with a spring clip, and add some plain hair grips to hold the twists firm if they try to unwind. Brush the untwisted hair smoothly down your back.

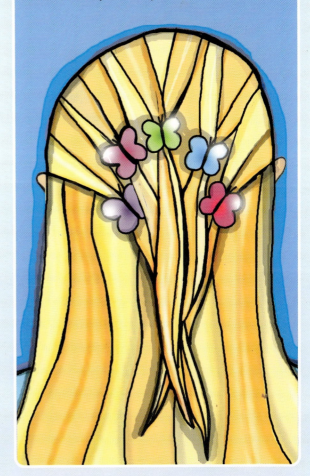

LET'S TWIST AGAIN

If you have a little more time, follow the instructions for Long and Lovely below, but take it a step further. Gather the ends of the twists into one hand as you go.

Then, without letting go of the ends, put a hairband round all the twists close to your head to form a ponytail. Twist this whole ponytail round and round until it forms a bun, and use hairpins or grips to hold this firm. You can decorate the twists with little clips if you like.

LOOKING LIVELY

Although light make-up looks best in the daytime, and flatters your face rather than drawing attention to it, it's great to go over the top if you have a big night out!

BRIGHT EYES

One golden rule of make-up is that you should have wild eyes, or brightly-coloured lips — but not both at once. If you use strong eye colours, like blue, green or purple, stick to natural-coloured lips. You can still use lots of clear lip gloss. Don't just use one eye colour all over. Practise with a pale highlighter over your lid and under your brow, then carefully sweep a small amount of darker colour at the corner of your lid. Use coloured eyeliner if you're feeling really brave!

PRECIOUS METALS

Gold and silver are perfect for a party look. You can use them on your eyes, cheeks, and even on your lips. Put on coloured lipstick as normal, and then use a small brush to dot a little gold or silver in the middle of your top and bottom lips. This will make your lips look full and pouty! Add some clear gloss over the top.

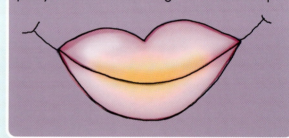

PRETTY PASTELS

Your make-up colours can be party-pretty without being dark. Extra pale, sparkly pinks and lilacs can look silly in the daytime, but are great for parties. Use shimmery highlighter on your cheekbones and glitter gel on your shoulders for a razzle dazzle makeover!

♥ TOP TIP

Practise wild make-up a couple of days before your party, so you don't have any disasters on the big night. Make sure you experiment in the right kind of lighting for the party — you don't want to look like a circus clown!

FUNKY ACCESSORIES

Any hairstyle looks even better if you decorate it with ribbons, gems or cute characters. If you can't find accessories in the shops that suit your style, why not make your own?

Sew tiny pompoms onto towelling hairbands to decorate a plain ponytail or bunches. You shouldn't need to use a very sharp needle. Ask an adult to thread an embroidery needle with ordinary cotton, and carefully poke it through the centre of the pompom and then through the hairband. Sew through the hairband at least twenty times before cutting off the thread.

Fake flowers are great for decorating your hair. Look in the shops for cheap, pretty versions that match your favourite outfits. Most of them have plastic or wire stems that you can poke straight into your hair, around a bun or high ponytail. If they have bendy wire, you can also wrap them carefully around bobbles and hair grips.

POP POMPOMS · FLOWER POWER · CUTE CREATURES · BEADS AND BOWS

Hunt around craft shops for beads in the shape of cute animals, and use them to decorate your hairdo. Thread embroidery thread through the centre, and knot it at each side to dangle the cuties from hair clips. You could also dab a small amount of strong glue onto the end of a cocktail stick and poke it part-way through the hole of the bead. Leave it to dry overnight, then ask an adult to cut off the remaining point. Poke the cocktail stick into the top of a bun so the creature peeps over the top!

Cut three pieces of embroidery thread the same length. Tie them together at the top and tape them to a notebook or kitchen cutting board. Start to plait them together for about 5cm. Then thread a bead onto the centre thread, or tie a small piece of ribbon in a bow around the centre thread. Carry on plaiting for 5cm and add another bead or ribbon. Tie a final knot about 5cm from the end of your plait, and use it to twist around a ponytail, or plait it into your own hair, fixing it with invisible hairbands.

17

PLENTY OF PLAITS

Learning to plait your hair is quite easy. Practise when you're watching TV and you'll soon get the hang of it! All the styles on these pages use plaits — just pick your favourite!

BASIC PLAIT

1 First, brush your hair until it's smooth, and separate the front section, from your ears forwards.

2 Divide this front section into three equal pieces. Hold them carefully so they all stay separate.

3 Take the lefthand section over the centre section. Take the righthand section over this new centre section.

♥ **TOP TIP**
Hold a small mirror behind your head as you look in your main mirror. You'll be able to see the back of your head, and check that your style is neat and in the centre.

4 Now you're plaiting! Keep plaiting the left section over the centre, then the right, and so on.

5 Keep plaiting to the end of your hair, then gather the ends together and hold them in place with a hairband.

HOLDING BACK

Use two plaits to make this pretty style. First brush your hair and separate a small section at each side, in front of your ears. Hold one section with a clip while you work on the other side. Divide this into three and plait neatly. Use a hairband to hold the plait securely. Unclip the other side and plait it in the same way. Loosely tie the two thin plaits behind your head, and hold them in place with a pretty clip.

ALL CHANGE

You can change this style by tying back your hair in bunches or a ponytail. Leave some plaits loose by your face if you like.

To fasten tiny, pretty beads into your plaits, you'll need more invisible hair-bands. Thread one through the hole in the centre of the bead, and loop it over so that first one end, then the other, wraps right around the plait and back over the bead to hold it in place.

PLAIT-O-RAMA!

This style is perfect to do when you're chilling out in front of the TV, but do check it in a mirror before you venture outside! You can do it on straight or curly hair, as long as it reaches your shoulders.

First, comb a neat centre parting into your hair. Then simply pinch small sections (about 2cm wide) from your parting and plait them neatly to the ends, fastening each with a tiny hairband.

SIXTIES STYLE

This simple style is created just by parting your hair in the centre and then plaiting each side. Accentuate the bottom of your plaits with cool ribbons or beads.

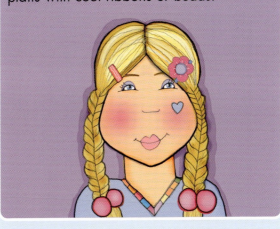

♥ TOP TIP
If your hair is flyaway or full of static, just spray a tiny amount of hairspray onto your brush or comb and run it through your hair. Instantly calmer!

TWO IN ONE

Sometimes, pulling long hair back to plait it behind your neck doesn't suit your face. This style is good to try instead, as it's softer and prettier. It's still quite easy to do, although you have to work neatly.

1 Brush your hair until it's smooth. Take a small section of hair from over your left ear, making sure all the hair from the front is neatly gathered in.

2 Divide this section into two equal strands. Twist one over the other, pulling the strands gradually back behind your ear as you twist.

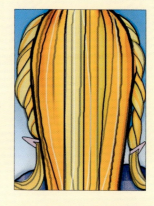

3 Near the bottom of the section, stop twisting and clip the hair firmly by your neck for the moment. Now do the same on the other side to make a second neat twist.

4 Divide your untwisted hair into three sections. Make the middle section slightly larger than the outside ones.

5 Gather up the left twist with the left section, and the right twist with the right section, and make a neat plait using the middle section as well. Fasten with a bobble.

♥ TOP TIP
If your twists come undone before you've finished the style, ask a friend to hold them tightly for you while you separate your hair to plait it.

BIG HAIR

This style will DEFINITELY get you noticed, so save it for a special occasion and prepare to stand out from the crowd! The style works on most types of hair, as long as it reaches your shoulders at least.

1 Make a neat centre parting all the way from your forehead to the back of your hair at the neckline. Loosely tie the righthand section by your ear to keep the parting in place.

2 Working on the lefthand section, take small pieces of hair and plait them to the very ends. Make lots of tiny plaits all through the section, but leave some of the hair loose as well.

3 Gather the hair into a neat ponytail over your ear. Use a large bobble to hold it in place, and make sure several of the plaits show around the outside of the ponytail.

4 Rub a little hair gel or wax onto the ponytail, and fluff it out to make it as big and bouncy as possible. Allow the ends of some plaits to start coming loose.

5 Repeat on the other side, making sure that the two ponytails are balanced and level. You don't want to look lop-sided!

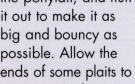

♥ TOP TIP
This style is a great one to combine with the Funky Girl hair mascara hints from page 26.

21

ON THE SIDE

This style is so cool even pop stars copy it for photoshoots! It looks as though it might take ages or be too tricky, but with a little practice (and maybe a helping hand for the back where you can't see!) you'll soon master it.

1 Brush your hair and make a parting slightly to one side. Brush the hair backwards and sideways into a ponytail. Fasten with a hairband.

2 Separate three tiny sections of hair and plait them. If you're not sure how to make plaits, check the instructions on page 18.

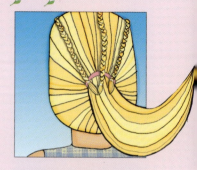

♥ **TOP TIP**
Don't wash your hair before styling it as washing it will make it too floppy and shiny to stay in place properly. Leave it for a day or two for much better results.

3 Make two or three more skinny plaits using tiny pieces of hair combed from your ponytail. Hold each one in place with an invisible hairband.

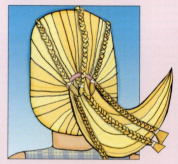

4 Gather together the ponytail with the plaits and twist the whole lot over and over, like a bun. Don't worry about the ends poking out.

5 Use hair pins and grips to hold the twist in place. Add a tiny amount of wax to the ends to make them stick out and look cool.

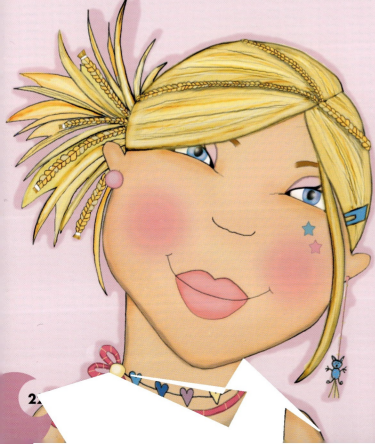

FUN FOR FINGERS

Your nails don't have to be very long to look lovely. Eat healthy foods (such as fruit, vegetables and cheese), keep them clean and unbitten, and they'll look great. You can use these ideas to make them perfect for parties!

PAINTING NAILS

1 Remove any old nail varnish using cottonwool soaked in gentle nail varnish remover. Wash your hands in warm soapy water.

2 If you don't want to paint your nails again, apply lots of hand cream. Don't do this if you want to varnish them now.

To paint cute flowers on your nails, dip the end of a cocktail stick into brightly coloured varnish, and paint each petal carefully. Finish with a dot of colour in the centre of each flower. Always wait until the first colour is dry before applying a new colour.

These hearts and stars look difficult, but are easy if you take your time. Again, use the point of a cocktail stick to paint tiny shapes. First, dot silver or red circles onto a nail with the varnish brush. Then drag the dot into the shape of a star, or a heart, with your cocktail stick.

3 To apply varnish neatly, paint one stripe up the centre of a nail, then a stripe at each side to fill the whole nail.

4 Let this colour dry for at least an hour, then use clear varnish to protect it, or copy the cool designs here.

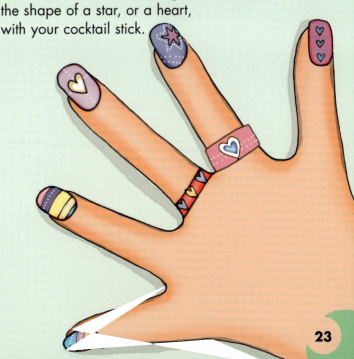

23

FUN IN THE SUN

Summertime is a great time to wear little or no make-up, keep your hairstyle as simple as possible, and enjoy getting out and about in the fresh air and sunshine. The sun provides your body with Vitamin D, which is great for your teeth, bones and skin.

Not Too Much!

Although the sun can help you feel great, and it's definitely good for you to be out in the open air when the weather is fine, too much is as bad as too little. Everyone should be aware that the sun can burn. It can damage your hair, your eyes and, worst of all, your skin. In the long term, too much sun can cause serious harm to your health. In the short term, sunburn is *really* painful, and sun stroke will make you feel *really* poorly.

♥ Top Tip

The sun can burn you even if it is cloudy and you are wearing light clothing. It's hottest between 11am and 3pm, so try to stay under the shade of a beach brolly or trees when the sun is high in the sky.

Vital Equipment

To protect your skin, you need to wear suntan lotion. Read the label carefully before you buy any. It needs to say that the lotion protects against UVA *and* UVB rays. It also needs an SPF (Sun Protection Factor) number of at least 15, but preferably 25 or 30.

Put lotion all over your body before you go out in the morning, to let it soak into your skin before the sun gets anywhere near it. Re-apply it after you get wet, from swimming, washing or playing in the water. Even if you don't get wet, add more lotion to your 'bare bits' every two hours.

FACE FACTS

Your face is likely to get burnt more easily than other parts of your body. Use a special sun block with a really high SPF number. Make sure you use it on your lips, nose and the tips of your ears as these burn first. Wear sunglasses to stop yourself screwing up your eyes in the bright light. Whenever possible, wear a hat, too, to protect the top of your head and the back of your neck. Constant sunshine on these parts will give you sunstroke which makes you feel sick, tired and no fun at all.

♥ TOP TIP

If you can't bear the thought of spending your holiday time with no make-up at all, keep it to a minimum. Some make-up ingredients may even make you more likely to burn. Stick to a slick of waterproof mascara and a coloured lip balm with a clear sun block over the top. Burnt, chapped lips look a hundred times worse than plain, uncoloured ones!

HAIR CARE

A hat doesn't just protect you from sunburn and sunstroke, it stops your hair becoming super-dry and frizzy with damaged ends. If you take your hat off to play sports, or go swimming, put suntan lotion on your parting to stop it from getting scorched. Pull your hair out of the way in a simple ponytail, or try the groovy style on page 28.

In hot weather, wash your hair every day, using a really gentle shampoo for frequent washing. This will stop your hair building up a nasty mixture of sweat, greasy lotion, chlorine and salt. Yuck! Make sure you use conditioner after every wash, too, as the sun may well make your hair drier than normal.

FUNKY GIRL

Don't just follow the crowd! You can use make-up on your hair and jewels on your face. Remember to check first that any glue or colour is suitable for your skin and will come off with soap and water.

HAIR FLAIR

You can add colour to your hair without scary permanent colour kits or trips to the hairdresser. Cheap and cheerful hair mascaras are easy to use. Separate small strands of hair and just stroke the mascara wand from the root to the tip to add some colour. Use it just in your fringe, or put highlights all over your top layer. Try just dabbing it on the tips of a flicked-out style.

FIX IT

If you have coloured hair pieces, tie them into a ponytail to make it harder to see where the fake hair joins your real hair. Or make a parting about 1cm from your normal parting. Fix the hair pieces in place (they're usually attached to a comb or hair grips). Then carefully make your usual parting and brush the hair over the top to hide where the colours join.

EASTERN CHARM

Some cultures use jewels as special face decorations. Bindis are especially pretty, and easy to use. Most have a sticky back so you can pop them in place straight onto your skin. Position the bindi carefully between your eyebrows. Use a coloured eyeliner pencil to add small dots at each side. Take the dots to just above your eyebrows, or all the way over your brows to the edges.

BEDAZZLED

Sparkle gel can be used on your body or on your face to add shimmer around your eyes and cheekbones. Look for gel with larger shapes in, such as sequins and stars, and position them one by one exactly where you want them. It's handy to use tweezers to get the tiny shapes exactly in position. Make a shooting star pattern down one cheek using a silver eye liner.

PARTY, PARTY

This isn't a great style for school every day, but it's worth the extra time if you're going to a party or somewhere extra special. Even though it's time-consuming, it's not really difficult to do.

> ♥ **TOP TIP**
> You might get aching arms doing this style yourself! Ask your mum or a friend to do it for you if they have the time to spare.

1 Smooth your hair back into a neat ponytail in the middle of your head (not too high or too low). Fasten with a plain hairband.

3 Keep twisting even more and the hair will start to coil around itself in a crazy loop. Let it wind itself towards your head, and fasten the end near your hairband using a hair grip.

2 Separate a small section of hair and hold it near the end. Twist it round and round until it becomes like a piece of rope.

4 Twist all of your hair in small sections in the same way. For a real party piece, thread glitter thread or ribbon in and out of the loops.

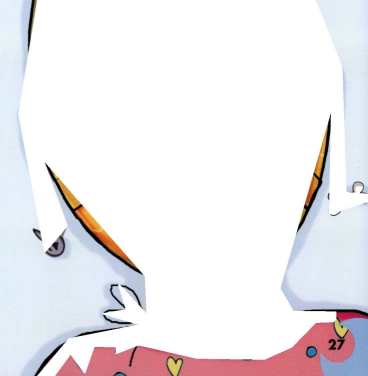

27

GET SET FOR SUMMER

If you're spending a lot of time outdoors in the summer, the sun could dry and damage your hair. Follow the tips on page 24, or keep your hair in good condition with this style.

♥ TOP TIP
Squirt the whole style with oil-free sun lotion (at least SPF 15) to keep your hair healthy and stop your scalp from getting burnt!

1 Make a neat parting just slightly off-centre. Use a clip to keep the right side out of the way for now, and brush the left side smooth.

2 Take a section of loose hair from the front and divide it into three equal sections. Plait them once. Then gather up a small section of loose hair and include it with the next strand to be plaited.

3 Keep doing this, adding a small section of loose hair with each section as you plait it. Guide the plait in a neat line over your ear, towards the back of your head. This style of plaiting is called French plaiting.

4 When all the loose hair is used up, simply keep plaiting until you get to the end and fasten with a bobble. Do just the same on the other side.

MEHNDI MAGIC

You don't have to pile lots of make-up on your face to look special for a party. Mehndi is the Asian art of body painting, and there are lots of beautiful patterns you can use to look special. Here are some Indian-inspired designs to copy.

1 To draw an armband or anklet, start with a simple wiggly line.

2 Add curls on some of the up or down waves.

3 Make the whole design thicker, then add dots above and below the original line.

4 For pretty flower patterns, start with a basic "fish hook" shape (like a T with looped top lines). Draw four in a cross shape.

5 Join the fish hooks together to make a real flower, or leave gaps between and add wiggly lines. Decorate with more dots or leaves.

> ♥ **TOP TIP**
> Buy a special body-art pen from a high street chemist and practise using it on a piece of skin that won't show if you make mistakes! Alternatively, use an eyeliner pencil with a good point for a design that lasts just a couple of hours.

CRAZY LADY

This style can take quite a long time to do, so save it for a night in with your friends, and ask them to help with some of the plaiting. It should stay neat even overnight, so you can leave it in for a few days after all your hard work!

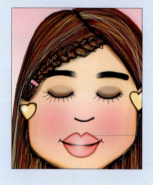   

1 Start by plaiting the front section of hair to keep it away from your face. Plait over to one side and fasten the end with a coloured band.

2 Separate another section of hair on top of your head, from one ear to the centre. French plait this section, taking in small strands of hair and working down to your ear.

3 Fasten the plait with a different coloured band. Do the same on the other side, French plaiting the hair down towards your ear. Hold firmly with a coloured band.

4 Separate the rest of your hair into sections and plait each one neatly. French plait as many sections as you can, and use normal plaits for the longer sections at your neck.

💗 **TOP TIP**
When plaiting, hold the hair in the direction it will eventually lie, to stop the plait sticking out of your head at a peculiar angle!

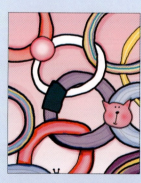

5 Fasten each plait with a different coloured band, and wear your brightest top to match!

MERMAID BRAIDS

If you've got really long, straight hair and are bored with wearing it in a ponytail or plaits all the time, try this fabulous style. It's practical enough for school but stylish enough to grab everyone's attention.

1 Make a neat centre parting and brush your hair smooth at each side. Spray a small amount of hairspray onto your brush first to keep any fine ends in place.

4 Carry on like this, working from the back then front each time, until you start to see your mermaid braid take shape. Tie it off at the bottom with a hairband or bobble.

2 Start work on the left side. Divide the hair into two equal sections. Then separate a small strand from the back of the back section, and take it over to join the front strand.

5 Do the same on the other side to make a second braid the same length as the first.

3 Take a small strand from the front of the front section, and cross it over to join the back strand.

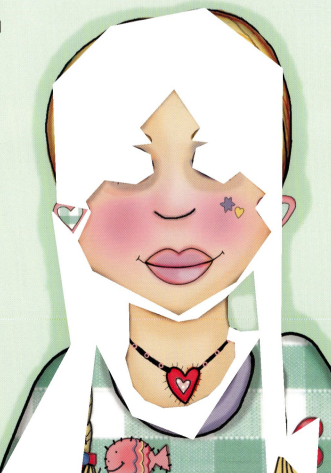

YOU GO, GIRL!

Wow! I hope you feel special on the inside, because with all these ideas to try you're sure to look stunning on the outside!

HERE'S LOOKING AT YOU

Some of the styles in this book are suitable for every day. Some of the styles are a bit too much for the daytime, though! Don't turn up at school with blue streaks in your hair and glitter all over your face. People may look twice, but they could end up laughing (or making you stay in at breaktime to do extra work!)

A NEW LOOK

If you're quite shy and daren't try out a new look, practise the style or make-up at home until you're more confident. It's a good idea to try a change of style when you're on holiday, so people don't know the "regular" you. Keep thinking, "I like it, so other people will as well." Don't worry if your brother laughs at you — after all, what does he know?

KISS

No, I'm not talking about boyfriends! KISS stands for "Keep It Sweet and Simple". Don't do too much at once, and don't think that complicated styles and make-up are necessarily best. If your fingernails are chewed and your breath smells, people may not hang around long enough to spot that your hair is a work of art.

FIRST, SECOND, THIRD IMPRESSIONS

It's true that first impressions count, but if someone sticks around long enough to talk to you, they'll also be interested in what you've got to say. Everyone you meet is a possible new friend, so be nice (even if you're feeling grumpy) and others will be nice to you!